WHAT IS
Christianity

WHAT IS
Christianity

WHO ARE THE CHRISTIANS

EDWARD E. STACKS

Charleston, SC
www.PalmettoPublishing.com

What is Christianity
Copyright © 2023 by Edward E. Stacks

All rights reserved
No portion of this book may be reproduced, stored in a retrieval system, or transmitted in any form by any means–electronic, mechanical, photocopy, recording, or other– except for brief quotations in printed reviews, without prior permission of the author.

First Edition

Paperback ISBN: 979-8-8229-1318-9

Table of Contents

Who Are the Christians?	1
What Christianity Is Not: a Religion	5
Who Is Jesus Who Was Called the Christ?	9
False Teachers and Preachers	25
The Reinvention of Christianity	27
Who Are the Christians?	31
The Call of God	33
Why So Many Different Groups (Denominations)?	35
Do Christians Believe in the Ten Commandments?	39
The Cross and the Christian Life	43
The Great Commission	47
The Reinvention of Christianity	51
What Is the Bible for in the Lives of Young People?	55
Conclusion	63

Who Are the Christians?

∝

In the world today, 50 percent of people profess to be Christians. Sixty-one percent of Americans profess to be Christians. In the UK just under 50 percent describe themselves as Christians. In Russia 79.4 percent say that they are Christians. In Ukraine 87.5 percent claim Christianity as their way to God. And at the same time, many of the nations of the world are involved in some kind of conflict with other nations that also may be Christian. Russia and Ukraine are, as of the writing of this book, involved in a full-scale war—two nations, each with populations that predominantly identify as Christian.

It is difficult to understand, with so many Christians and so much Christian influence, how so much war could be going on with professing Christians on every side of a conflict.

So what's going on? Isn't Jesus called the "Prince of Peace"? If He is, and if their relationship with Him is real, then what is wrong?

The answer is that almost anywhere we may find two or more "believers," it is likely that we will find just about that many definitions of the word "Christian." Many call themselves Christians who have no knowledge at all of what Christianity is or who Christians are. It would seem that there is no absolute definition or, at least, no absolute guidelines to tell us what is real and what is not.

But there is an absolute. And that is what this book is about. There is only one standard by which the question can be accurately answered. That standard is Jesus Christ: His life, His teachings, His death, and His resurrection. When we want to know what Christianity is like, we must look at Him. No other standard will do. And His life is recorded in the pages of a book called the Bible.

But many other standards have been offered up, and at the time of the writing of this book, Christianity is in the process of being reinvented. Some seem to believe that Christianity must be made more palatable to the taste of people of the current generation—they fail! Christianity is what it has always been with no change allowed! "Christ in you, the hope of glory" (Col 1:27 NIV) is still the base of it all. And that will never change. Christianity is the person of Jesus Christ living in His people.

Everything else changes; God said, "I am the Lord, I change not" (Mal 3:6 KJV). Christianity does not have to be learned over and over and over. Like God Himself, it changes not. Once we learn it, we've got it. And yes, there is so much to be learned—so much about Jesus and those who are His people.

Christians are not perfect people. They are people on a journey. Their standards are very high, for their goal is to be like their Lord. And it is this that often gives rise to the charge of hypocrisy, for they do fall short of the standard, and there is always someone watching...often just to try and catch them in a fall.

The journey is called "sanctification," and it is the process by which God removes things from their lives that ought not to be there and adds things that ought to be there. And the standard is so high that the process continues until the day they go to be with Him.

Christians are defined by their personal relationship to Jesus Christ.

Christianity is defined by the journey that Christians all must travel.

This book is about all of that, as the Holy Spirit leads in putting it together.

"And Agrippa replied to Paul 'Are you trying to persuade me to become a Christian?'" (Acts 26:28). "Let none of you suffer as a murderer or a thief or an evildoer or as a meddler into others' affairs; but as if a Christian, let him not be ashamed, but let him glorify God in this name of Jesus" (1 Pet 4:16).

The word "Christian" appears in the New Testament only two times. Christians are called, or referred to as, disciples almost 250 times in the New Testament. A disciple is someone who learns from someone else; Christians are people who learn from Jesus. Because of Him and our allegiance to Him, we use the name "Christian."

Christianity is often referred to as a religion. "Religion" is a word with many different meanings to many different people. It can be brought down to "any form or organization that seeks to know God, please God, and go to Heaven all on the basis of what they can do in order to achieve those objectives." It promises blessings now and eternal life in the future based solely on what one may do to earn those blessings.

What Christianity Is Not: a Religion

There is something in the world today that many refer to as the "Christian religion." The Christian religion is a deadly enemy of biblical Christianity because, at first glance, it looks so much like the real thing. The essential similarity is that the Christian religion has adopted many of the teachings of Christ, but with no personal relationship with Him, there is no personal presence of Christ in their assemblies. The Christian religion is basically the methods, values, and principles of the world system wrapped up in Christian clothing. It is altogether without the presence or power of Jesus Christ.

The teachings of Jesus Christ are simply beyond comparison! And when applied according to directions, they will always bring about positive change, both individually and culturally. The problem with "religion" is that the teachings of Christ are ideal only when Christ Himself is the standard of reference as to whether a thing is right or wrong, good or bad, righteous or evil.

His teachings are so far above us that we, by our own abilities, just cannot keep them consistently and faithfully. There is, though, a power that comes straight from the Lord Jesus, and when that power gets hold of us, we can be and do what He wants. That power comes to believers through a person called Holy Spirit. He is the great enabler where the genuine Christian faith exists. "I can do all things through Christ who strengthens me" (Phil 4:13 NKJV). This is the basic mantra of all of Christians: all things through Christ.

About the person called Holy Spirit, Jesus said: "But the Comforter, the Holy Spirit, Whom the Father will send in My name, HE will teach you all things and remind you of all things which I said to you" (John 14:26). And then: "But I tell you the truth, it is expedient for you that I go away; for if I do not go away the Comforter will not come to you; but if I go I will send Him to you" (John 16:7). Note carefully that the Bible (in good translations) never ever refers to the Holy Spirit as "it." He is a person, not a thing.

If Christianity was just another religion, it would be embraced by most other religions; the thing that makes

Christianity different, and literally hated by many of the religions of the world, is something that Jesus said: "I am the way and the truth and the life. No one comes to the Father except through me" (John 14:6 NIV). This is fundamental in Christianity, and as hated as it may be by religion, it is the truth upon which Christianity stands! And it must never be compromised, not even a little bit! The definite article "the" means that He is not one of several, but the *only* one who is the way, truth, and life of God among men.

And it needs to be said that Christianity is not a political system; it is not a moral system (though it presents a moral system), it is not a philosophy of living; and it is not a set of rules. Christianity contains these things, but it is much, much more than these.

Who Is Jesus Who Was Called the Christ?

Christians have experienced Jesus's presence, His power, His providence, and His purpose, and enough for them. However, there is more: there are the written testimonies of first-person witnesses who saw Him in the flesh, and some of them lived with Him for as much as three and a half years. They saw the miracles and heard the teachings, and they were so convinced of His claims that they put their lives on the line in order to live for Him, and some of them, directed by Holy Spirit, wrote much of it down so that those of us who lived many years later could still get the truth. We call those writings the "Holy Bible."

John was a young man when Jesus called him to follow Him. He followed and lived with Jesus for several years. He wrote: "In the beginning was the Word, and the Word was with God, and the Word was God. He was in the beginning with God. All things came into being through Him, and apart from Him not one thing came into being which has come into being" (John 1:1–3).

There can be little doubt about what John was writing. Directed by the Holy Spirit of God, he told us that the great Creator actually became a man! Some try to explain this away; it doesn't work. It says what it means and means what it says: for a short period of time, the God of our creation became like one of us.

Then in chapter one, verse fourteen, John wrote, "And the Word became flesh and dwelt among us, and we beheld His glory, the glory as of the only begotten of the Father, full of grace and truth" (John 1:14 NKJV). The Word that became flesh was Jesus.

And then John wrote: "That which was from the beginning, which we have heard, which we have seen with our eyes, which we have looked upon and our hands have handled, concerning the Word of life—the life was manifested, and we have seen, and bear witness, and declare to you that eternal life which was with the Father and was manifested to us—that which we have seen and heard we declare to you, that you also may have fellowship with us" (1 John 1:1–3 NKJV).

John said: we heard His teachings, we saw Him day by day, we saw Him over a long period of time, and we touched Him. He was not a spirit, He was there with us as a man—*the* man.

Jesus is the one about whom John wrote and about whom the whole New Testament bears witness. Christians must not compromise the truth about who Jesus was (and is). Leaving out portions of the Word can be just as damaging as inserting opinions in place of truth. Jesus is the "only begotten Son of God" (John 3:18 NKJV), and Christians must never compromise this truth.

Christianity is not a religion; it is a faith. "Beloved, using all diligence to write to you of our common salvation, I have been obliged to write to you exhorting [you] to contend earnestly for the faith once delivered to the saints" (Jude 3 DARBY). Our faith is not in our goodness or our ability to do great things; our faith is solely placed in the One whom John and the other apostles wrote about.

Religion is all about our own efforts to find God; Christianity is about what Jesus did. Men always fall short; Jesus never did. By faith in Him, we have forgiveness of sins, blessings now in this life, and eternal life in the place He has prepared for us (see John 14).

Casual observation tells us that humanity has a problem. The Bible tells us what it is and how to fix it...but humans, as a whole, are not always very good at listening! We have tried hundreds of different religions, and they have not worked. But remember, Christianity is not a religion. So, the question is this: can Christianity fix the human problem?

First, we have to recognize what the problem is. Nobody wants to talk about it anymore or even use the word. But the Bible uses the word and tells us exactly what the human problem is: sin. Sin is demonstrably with us now and doing quite well. We have tried various religions, we have tried politics, we have signed contracts and agreements... all have failed. The problem has not changed.

There is an answer. Christianity is the answer—the *only* answer. And we must start by recognizing the fact that Christianity has simply not been tried on any large scale—that is, the Christianity that we find in the Bible. The Christian "religion" works no better than any other religion. But the Christian faith, whenever and wherever it is tried, works!

The theory of Christianity won't do. Only the actual presence of Jesus Christ in human life can repair the damage sin has done. Believe it! There is no other solution. Utopia will never come because of that one little word: *S-I-N*. Someone once said, "Christianity won't work." Fact: every place where true biblical Christianity has honestly been tried, it works! Every time! And where it is tried, it produces changed lives.

Christianity is not an elevated system of dos and don'ts. It is a life and a resultant lifestyle. One renowned leader of a world religion once said, "I could never become a Christian because I have never seen one who practices what he professes to believe."

So what does a real Christian look like? He is more than a rule keeper. There is something much deeper, something that touches the deepest part of his life. Something that changes not only his actions but also changes how he thinks, how he behaves, and much deeper than even that. It is a life devoted to the best life ever: a life following Jesus Christ in the "narrow road" (Matt 7:14 NIV).

It is, in its essence, Christ living out His life in us. "Christ in you, the hope of glory" (Col 1:27).

Once we know who Jesus is and the difference between Christianity and religion, we need now to know about the gospel of Jesus Christ. The word "gospel" comes from the word "evangelism." Evangelism is the good news that God loves us and has made a way for us to come to Him—not as a god somewhere, but as our Heavenly Father.

So what is the "good news"? "Good" must be measured against a backdrop of "bad." The bad news is that God is holy and we were created in His image and in His likeness. So far, so good. However, our first parents disobeyed the one commandment that He gave to them, and sin entered into the human race. God gave those first humans a choice. He had put trees in the Garden of Eden, and there was one tree that was forbidden. It was the tree of the knowledge of good and evil. They chose to be disobedient, thus breaking the fellowship with God that was intended. We must understand that a holy God insists that our lives move in the direction of His own likeness. And in our first parents, a different road was chosen. We were created for eternal life with Him in heaven, but disobedience changed all of that. Instead of life, death entered the world. We were not created to die! But human sin changed our destiny; instead of life we got death. That death meant eternal separation from the God who created us; once we saw what we had missed, we learned what hell is really like. The most painful thing of all is to be separated from the love of God forever and forever.

Then came the gospel of Jesus Christ. That which our first parents, and then we, messed up, Jesus came to restore.

God is God, and He has a plan to restore what we have lost. First, know that God is just, and what He says is the way that it is. When the apostle Paul said that "the wages of sin is death" (Rom 6:23 NIV), that is exactly what he meant. Second, know that God is also merciful, which can be understood through the word "propitiation" (1 John 4:10). Propitiation means someone stood up for us and took our punishment upon Himself, and that is exactly what Jesus did.

God requires the penalty be paid, and only someone without sin could pay the price for those who had sin. Propitiation means the mercy of God was given, and the justice of God was satisfied. Each of these, mercy and law, were satisfied in the death of Jesus Christ. Something happened on the cross that is beyond full explanation. "He became sin for us, who knew no sin, that we might become the righteousness of God in Him" (2 Cor 5:21). In those moments on the cross, Jesus "became sin" and in death paid the supreme penalty for human sin. The resurrection proved it all!

The whole story of the redemption that we now speak of is recorded for us in the Old Testament in the book of Exodus, chapter twelve—words written approximately 1,500 years before Christ was born. God brought a series of judgments against Egypt with the goal of forcing the Pharoah to release the Hebrews from 400 years of Egyptian captivity. After nine judgments the Hebrew slaves were still not free to leave Egypt. God would send one more judgment.

The Hebrews were to kill an *unblemished* lamb. They were to take the blood of the lamb and put some of it over the doors of their homes and some of it on the sides of the doorposts. This was the blood of an unblemished lamb, and God said, "When I see the blood, I will pass over you" (Ex 12:13).

This was the beginning of the Jewish Passover, and it graphically pictured the deliverance from the power of sin for all who would come to the cross of Jesus Christ and there put their lives "under the blood" of the true Lamb of God. The blood of Jesus Christ was shed for the remission of sin and required only that men look to the cross and to the sacrifice of Jesus in order to receive the deliverance that only the blood of the Lamb could bring. That look must be in faith in Jesus Christ and what He did on the cross. When John introduced Jesus to the public, he introduced Him as "the Lamb of God, who takes away the sin of the world" (John 1:29 NIV).

Because Christianity finds its life and meaning in Jesus, we need to know what kind of a man He was. That is important, because His character is exactly what God is working to produce in the lives of all Christians. And by looking carefully at the various events of His life and by a study of His words, we can answer the question; we can know about His human side and how He lived it. Looking at His life gives us an idea of where we are and how much we have grown in relation to the goal to be like Jesus.

Note: the writers of the New Testament were well aware of the dual nature of Jesus; He was, in the same body, God and man.

We need to be very careful here to understand that Christ was both God and man. In this book, the goal is to look at the human side: who He was as a man. And without trying too hard, we find over thirty places in the New Testament where we see the human side of Jesus. We will look at some of these.

1. First, He was always concerned to do the will of the Father. "Let this mind be in you which was also in Christ Jesus, who existing in the form of God did not consider being equal with God a treasure to be grasped, but emptied himself, taking the form of a slave, becoming in the likeness of men; and being found in fashion as a man, He humbled himself, becoming obedient even unto death, and that the death of a cross" (Phil 2:5–8).

Jesus was committed to know and do the will of the Father and to obey that will. Even if doing so would require Him to give His life on a cross. What an example! Christ is our Savior, and we all know that, but many apparently do not know that His life as a man established the ultimate example of how we should live. And in the scripture above, we are cautioned to "let" this mind be in us: a mind seeking to be obedient to the Father. *For Jesus, obedience led to death; for us, it leads to life.*

We need to understand that, in this life, perfection is simply beyond us. Imperfect people do not lead perfect lives. But we can and must seek it and be on the journey to it.

2. Jesus was always gracious in His relationships. "For you know the grace of our Lord Jesus Christ, that though He was rich, for your sakes He became poor, in order that you, because of His poverty might become rich" (2 Cor 8:9). Jesus left the glory of heaven in order to come to this little planet and to show us what life is truly about and then to pay the awful price of our sin on the cross. He became poor; in Him, we become rich. All because of His grace. Grace, by definition, means that God, through His Son, has given us something we could never deserve. The word for "grace" in the New Testament (*charis*) is the same as the word "gift." So when we talk about the grace of Jesus, we talk about the gift of Jesus: the free gift.

3. Jesus was altogether forgiving. One very good example of His kind of forgiveness took place when He was on the cross and in terrible pain. He looked at those who drove the nails into His hands and said, "Father, forgive them for they know not what they do" (Luke 23:34). The word that Jesus used for "forgive" was a word that means "to throw something away." Jesus was telling His Father to take these sins from these men and throw them away.

Another good example of the real meaning of Christianity is a living, loving spirit of forgiveness. And yes, real forgiveness never calls back those things that were thrown away.

4. Jesus was altogether loving. For Jesus, love was not just a word; it was a life with specific attitudes and actions. Words are OK, but without appropriate attitudes and actions, they mean little. Jesus said, "As the Father has loved Me, so have I loved you; continue ye in My love" (John 15:9). He also said, "Greater love has no man than this that a man lay down his life for his friends" (John 15:13). And finally, "In this we know love, that He laid down His life on our behalf, and we ought to lay down our lives on behalf of the bothers" (1 John 3:16).

Jesus's death on the cross is the single most significant event in human history. It was there He lived out what He had taught. And thousands and thousands of Christians have given their lives for each other and for the Kingdom of God. The single greatest need of humanity is peace with God. Peace is made possible only by what Jesus did on the cross.

Christianity, by biblical definition and example, is quite different from much of what we see in the world at this present time. Its standards are much, much higher than most understand. And we must not ever lower or in any way change those standards. God's goal for all of His children is Christlikeness, nothing less, nothing other. Only One has achieved obedience to those standards, but Christians must be living in such a way as to be more like Him today than we were a year ago.

5. Christ was compassionate. The English word "compassion" comes from a Greek word that speaks of a yearning from deep inside. The word "yearn" speaks to a deep, intense longing for someone. Jesus longed for all who were (and are) separated from God. "And a leper came to Him, entreating Him and falling on his knees, and saying to Him, if you are willing, you can cleanse me. And He was moved with compassion, and stretching out His hand, He touched him and said to him, I am willing, be cleansed" (Mark 1:40-41).

No one would think of touching a leper. But Jesus did! Jesus had that deep yearning for this man and touched and healed him.

Five times in the New Testament we find the phrase "and moved with compassion" (Matt 9:36; 14:14; 18:27; Mark 1:41; 6:34). Compassion is to be an identifying characteristic of a Christian as much as it was for Christ. Compassion always moves in a positive way toward someone in need, whether the need is spiritual or physical. He always moved toward human misery, and so must those who call Him Lord.

Character matters! And the character of Jesus matters most of all, for in the character of Jesus Christ, we find the meaning and definition of Christianity. Christ in us, the hope of glory.

6. Christ exemplified something called the "fruit of the Spirit" (Galatians 5:22-23). "But the fruit of the Spirit is love, joy, peace, long-suffering, kindness, goodness, faithfulness, meekness." The word "love" comes from the Greek "*agape*," and this word always speaks of God's kind of love, that is, a giving, caring, helping kind of love. Jesus has this love for us, and we now must have it for each other. "A new commandment I give to you, that you love one another, even as I have loved you, that you also love one

another. By this shall all men know that you are my disciples, if you have love for one another" (John 13:34–35).

So what is Christianity? What is a Christian? It is far more than how one acts; it is something inside that creates the character of Jesus Christ. It is a *relationship* with Jesus Christ that shows in one's behavior, one's thinking, and one's attitudes. Again, not perfection, but very much on the journey.

7. What about anger? Is it possible to be a Christian and still get angry? Yes. There are times and circumstances in which the only appropriate response is anger. It happened to Jesus; it will surely happen to His people. "And the Passover of the Jews was near, and Jesus went up to Jerusalem. And He found in the temple those selling oxen and sheep and doves, and the moneychangers sitting there. And having made a whip out of cords, He drove them all out of the temple, as well as the sheep and the oxen, and He poured out the money of the moneychangers and overturned their tables."

Can you see it? Jesus was angry! The temple of God was being violated, and He would not have it! Can you see gentle Jesus, meek and mild, throwing over the tables and driving the moneychangers out with a whip? Yes! Circumstances required it to be! And in every generation, at any time, circumstances such as these may arise. And Christians then must allow the example of Jesus to take over. There are, in this world, things that bring an appropriate anger response from those who know Jesus Christ.

It is critically important that Christians know when anger is appropriate or not. Anger, out of place, will hinder our witness to Christ, sometimes severely. Out of control, it can be extremely dangerous.

8. Did Jesus ever cry? Yes, Jesus cried (John 11:1-12). Crying is an emotional response that triggers a physical response. Tears came from Jesus when He stood at the tomb of His friend, Lazarus. He had been away, and Lazarus had been dead for four days when Jesus came. Friends of Lazarus were hurting because of the death of their friend, and in the case of Mary and Martha, their brother.

Jesus came, and two words describe His response to the crying and wailing that was happening. Two words describe Jesus's response. "He was moved with indignation, and was troubled in His spirit." The English equivalent of the Greek words indicates that Jesus was upset when He saw the crying and the tears, and He groaned in His Spirit. He was not troubled by the death of His friend, but by the pain the sisters and friends were experiencing. Literally

"He troubled Himself." And it was this kind of trouble that moved Him to tears.

Death always has a different look when Jesus is present! There are times for crying, and there are times and occasions for rejoicing. Jesus wept, but all weeping was gone when Lazarus came out of the tomb.

9. Jesus epitomized the love of God. His love was *unconditional*. He loved when He knew it would not be returned. He loved when there would be a price to be paid. Christ's love was *self-sacrificing*. He put His life on the line for His friends (John 15:13). His love for us was and is *inseparable*. "Who shall separate us from the love of Christ? Shall tribulation, anguish, persecution, or famine, or nakedness, or peril or sword? In all of these things we are *more than conquerors*, through Him who loved us" (Rom 8:35-37). Jesus's love was giving. "He loved the church and gave Himself for it" (Eph 5:25). And His love was *forgiving*. He even forgave those who beat Him and mocked Him, who spit on Him, and who nailed Him to the cross! Note that His forgiveness was complete. So must ours be.

False Teachers and Preachers

In defining Christianity, we need to know what Jesus said about false shepherds, false prophets, and false teachers. These are the people who make the "Christian religion" look like the real thing, though it isn't.

False shepherds "see the wolf coming and leave the sheep and flee, and the wolf catches them and scatters them" (John 10:12). They are pretenders: men who do not know Jesus Christ, but who infiltrate the church and allow heresies to thrive.

False prophets are similar. "And many false prophets will arise and will lead many astray (Matt 24:11). Satan is real, and he hates everything that God loves. He hates the church of Jesus Christ, and he would destroy it if he could. And he is good at what he does! Heresy (false doctrine) is destructive. And much like cancer, if it is not dealt with, it will destroy whatever it touches. These are preachers who compromise the Word of God for personal advancement.

False teachers are those who distort the Word of God. "These people honor me with their lips, but their heart strays far away from me; in vain do they worship me teaching as teachings the teachings of men" (Matt 15:8-9). It only takes a little poison to ruin the water supply of a large city. So it is with those who stray from the Word of God in favor of personal opinions.

The Reinvention of Christianity

There are those who contend that Paul invented Christianity. Not so. Paul was an instrument in the hands of God to write all that he wrote. "For I make known to you brothers, concerning the Gospel announced to me, that it is not according to man. For neither did I receive it from man, nor was I taught it, but I received it through a revelation by Jesus Christ (Gal 1:11-12). Paul's writings were consistent with the whole body of his writings, and his writings were consistent with everything that Jesus said.

The four Gospels tell the story of Jesus; the epistles (the letters of Paul, Peter, James, and John) give us a clear and final revelation of His message to the world. Paul would take no credit for inventing Christianity. He understood that he was merely the instrument and that the words were words from God Himself.

So what do I mean when I talk about the "reinvention" of Christianity? Four things stand out: 1) some things have been added to the Word; 2) some things have been deleted; 3) some things have been changed; and 4) some things have been left out.

1. Things added: The Bible makes becoming a Christian so simple that no one will miss heaven because of a lack of understanding. Over and over, the Bible tells us that in order to become a Christian, one must call on the name of the Lord: "For whoever calls upon the name of the Lord shall be saved (Rom 10:13). And "Jesus said to her [Martha], 'I am the resurrection and the life; he who believes in Me, even If he should die, shall live'" (John 1:25). Over and over Scripture tells us that the condition of salvation is to "believe" in Jesus Christ. To believe something is to accept it as fact, as truth. Fact: Jesus's death on the cross paid the price of sin, and in believing in that death, He forgives and puts our names in the Lamb's book of life. Some have added a long list of things that one must do in order to be "saved"; the Bible knows only one. Now, having said that, we need to remember

that once the baby is born, there are things that must happen in order for the baby to develop. It is exactly that way in the Christian life. We are born into the Christian life by faith in Him; now we must learn what this new life is all about, and it will be quite different from what we have left. A major part of the church and its gifts is to help and encourage new believers to live what they now have in Christ.

2. Things deleted: The need for confession and forgiveness. Sin in any of its forms will break one's fellowship with God. The way back is simple but often ignored: "If we say that we do not have sin we are deceiving ourselves and the truth is not in us. If we confess our sins he is faithful and righteous to forgive us our sins and cleanse us from all unrighteousness." Real confession works! Confession means "I did it, and no one else is to blame." (See 1 John 1:8–9.)

3. Some things have been changed: I've heard it said, "I don't go to church; I am the church." This is terrible, but it is happening. By definition, the church is a "called-out assembly." It is a gathering with God-chosen men to operate it. Deacons do not operate the church, and neither does congregational vote. And all believers are called by God to get into that

fellowship: "God is faithful through whom you were called into the fellowship of His Son Jesus Christ (Col 1:9). The local assembly is that fellowship.

4. Things that are often left out: personal responsibility and accountability. In his book *The Cost of Discipleship*, Dietrich Bonhoeffer calls this "cheap grace." These things have been left out for so long that anyone who preaches or teaches them is often called a heretic. These things must return to the Christian vocabulary.

Who Are the Christians?

First, and most importantly, Christians are "Christ in you, the hope of glory" (Col 1:27 NIV).

Christians are what they believe: Jesus Christ is the Son of God. He was the required sacrifice for sin. In Him and in Him alone do we find forgiveness for sin. In Him and Him alone do we find the truth about ourselves, our lives, and God.

Christians are how they live. In Acts 1:8, Jesus said that His people would be His witnesses, and He used the word *marturion* to describe them. *Marturion* is the word for "martyr." A martyr is one who chooses "death over denial."

Christians are the people for whom Jesus Christ is not only Savior, but also Lord.

They recognize that their personal relationship with Him is the single most important thing in all of life.

Some are mature believers, and some are babies. Some demonstrate what they believe better than others. They are all on the same journey.

The Call of God

No definition of Christianity would be complete without knowing something about the call of God.

The word "call" speaks of causing someone to have a strong urge to choose a particular career or way of life. Such is the call of God. God impresses us in such a way as to create a strong urge to follow Him in a particular way. God calls, and wise men answer. Here are several comments regarding the call of God:

There is God's call to all to come to Himself through His Son to a particular kind of life. That life is one of allegiance to Jesus Christ as Lord (owner) and Savior (payment for sin). And there is allegiance to the Bible, the written Word of the living God. To hold it close and to take advantage of every opportunity to search out and learn its truths. In His prayer in John 17, Jesus prayed for us that we would be sanctified (mature, grow up). He said, "Sanctify them in truth, thy word is truth" (John 17:17). So in order to grow up in Christian maturity, we must have a strong allegiance to the Bible, the written Word of God.

Christians will always have a sense of responsibility and accountability. The more mature they are, the more those things will show up. This is a place in which the church has a serious responsibility to the believer.

Christians grow in relationships with other people, especially those of the faith. Christians are called to a life of love: love for the Body of Christ and also for those who do not know Christ. It is the love of God working in Christians that makes Christians different. Again, the more mature they are, the more this will show up.

Christians have joined a new family: the family of God. Everyone who has come to Jesus Christ in faith has become a part of the one Body of Christ. We are all brothers and sisters.

Then there will be the consciousness of sitting at the feet of Jesus to know Him better and better.

There is then a call of God to some within the Body to a special kind of service. This call comes from His sovereignty and not because of merit. It is a call of pure grace.

Why So Many Different Groups (Denominations)?

Again, if all Christians are a part of the one Body of Christ, and if they relate to one another on the basis of love, grace, and forgiveness, why are there so many different denominations, often arguing with one another, seldom really working together to win the world to Jesus Christ? Why? There is, often, even a spirit of competition among them. Again, why?

The church has lost much of its witness today. The cause is not difficult to discern: we are presenting a jigsaw-puzzle Jesus! The lost world has a right to ask why. Just a few years ago, approximately 70 percent of Americans said they belonged to and attended a church. Perhaps not regularly, but at least they attended. As of this date (2-11-03) that number has changed radically to just 50 percent. We are losing ground in the Great Commission.

The Lord Jesus wants the world to see an accurate presentation of Christianity. And the lost world needs to see it! And He chose the church to present the real picture of Christianity. And the divisions in the Body just don't do it.

In John chapter 17 we find Jesus's high-priestly prayer. And in it we find these words: "And the glory which You have given Me I have given to them, that they may be one, even as we are one; I in them and You in me, that they may be perfected into one, that the world may know that you have sent me and have loved them even as You have loved Me" (John 17:22–23).

This passage leads to the first function of Christianity and the Christian Church: a Christian is someone who cares about those who are outside the Kingdom of God.

Christians have a desire to see others come to faith in Jesus. They love to give their testimony as to how they came to Christ themselves. And it is their oneness that tells the world who Jesus is!

There must be a way and a time in which the various denominations understand what our divisions have cost in terms of reaching people for Christ. Sometimes important things have to be put aside in favor of critical things! Don't give up the important; just don't allow it to separate the Body! The list of critical things in our belief system is short:

1. The virgin birth of Jesus Christ

2. The sinless life of Jesus

3. The vicarious/substitutionary atonement through the cross

4. The resurrection of Jesus Christ

5. His sure and certain return for His "kids"

6. The absolute reliability of the Bible, the written Word of the Living God

Christians' deep desire is to be obedient to the Lord Jesus, who gave them their marching orders as they are recorded in Matthew 28:19-20. "Go, therefore and disciple all the nations, baptizing them into the name of the Father and the Son, and of the Holy Spirit Teaching them to observe all that I have commanded you. And behold I am with you all the days until the consummation of the age."

Christianity says that everyone must have the opportunity to come to Jesus in order receive the life that He has to give, life with meaning and purpose and power and eternity with Him in the prepared place (see John 14).

Christians believe in eternal life in the place Jesus has prepared for us (see John 14). They also believe there is another prepared place for those who willingly reject Jesus Christ. Matthew 25:41 speaks of a place prepared for "the devil and his angels."

Yes, Christians do believe that there is an enemy of God, and his name is Satan. He is real. In the book of Revelation he is called "Abaddon" and "Apollyon," each word meaning "destroyer" (Rev 9:11).

Do Christians Believe in the Ten Commandments?

In order to answer whether Christians believe in the Ten Commandments, we would have to pick out those we do not believe in. And we can't find even one. The problem that Christians see with the Old Testament is not its teachings; it is about having salvation based on the keeping of the laws of God.

In the book of Acts, we are privileged to see the apostles and elders of the Church as they made a critically important decision: do Gentiles have to keep the Law of Moses in order to be saved?

The answer: "Therefore why are you now testing God by placing a yoke upon the neck of the disciples, which neither our fathers nor we were able to bear? But we believe that through the grace of our Lord Jesus we are saved in the same way also as they are" (Acts 15:10-11).

The apostles knew that the law of God was good, but they also knew that no one had ever kept the law perfectly. Enter grace: the God who gave the law also gave grace! The law revealed the sinfulness of all of humanity. In that sense, the law condemned. So by law revealing our sin, we discovered the need for grace. And grace came to the human race through the Lord Jesus and His death on the cross. And by no other means!

Returning to the Ten Commandments, they become a guide for living a godly life.

I. One God; His name is Jehovah (Jer 16:21)

II. No "graven images," no handmade items to worship

III. Do not take the name Jehovah in vain, carelessly

IV. Remember the Sabbath day; keep it holy; rest and worship

V. Highly esteem your parents—a commandment with a promise (Ex 20:12)

VI. You shall not kill (literally "murder"); the only truly innocent among us are unborn babies

VII. Sex was a design of God, and so was marriage; they must go together

VIII. No stealing

IX. No lying or giving false testimony

X. No coveting (heart attitude toward the possessions of others); coveting often precedes and encourages other sins

So what did Jesus have to say about it? "Do not think that I have come to abolish the law or the prophets, I have come not to abolish but to fulfill" (Matt 5:17).

In order to explain what He meant, He said, "Therefore whoever annuls one of the least of these commandments, and teaches men so, shall be called the least in the kingdom of heaven; but whoever practices them and teaches them, he shall be called great in the kingdom of heaven" (Matt 5:19).

The implication is clear: sin begins in the heart of a man. If it is not dealt with in its beginnings, it continues in outward actions

The Cross and the Christian Life

So many songs and so many Bible verses are all dedicated to one thing: the cross upon which Jesus died under the judgment of His Father for the sin of all mankind! One verse that escapes the attention of most is this one: "He became for us, who knew no sin, that we might become the righteousness of God in Him" (2 Cor 5:21).

There are some absolutes—things that are there and do not change, no matter the times or the circumstances or anything else. What happened at the cross on that day is absolute in all of the universe; it will never be changed, not even a little bit.

Many hate the cross. Why? Because, as Jesus said, their deeds are evil and they do not come to the light, lest they be exposed as sinners! And a close encounter of this kind will change a man's life fully.

Here is what the cross means and what happened.

"All have sinned," and the "wages of sin is death" (Rom 3:23; 6:23). But the "gift of God is eternal life in Christ Jesus our Lord" (Rom 6:23). But the wage that sin owes has to be paid! It is an absolute of the eternal God. All sin and all die, unless God had or has a plan to annul the payment. He did have such a plan!

Now notice this: the judgment of God requires the penalty to be paid! And that penalty is death. But there is another factor: the mercy of God is also an absolute! God is just, and God is merciful. So how can both law and mercy/grace be satisfied? Humanly speaking, it cannot happen, but God is not bound by human inabilities. He had a plan. He Himself would pay that price! But only a sinless man could do that! And where could He find a sinless man?

There would be only One who could do it: God's only begotten Son. But He was not a man. How could it be? The only answer: that only begotten Son must become a man Himself! And He did!

"Let this mind be in you which was also in Christ Jesus: Who existing in the form of God, did not consider being equal with God a treasure to be grasped, but emptied himself taking the form of a slave, becoming in the likeness of men; and being found in fashion as a man, He humbled himself, becoming obedient even unto death, and that the death of a cross" (Phil 2:5-8). He came here! Why? God loves His created ones—so much that He gave His only begotten Son, "that whosoever would believe in him, would not perish but have everlasting life" (John 3:16).

God loves. Jesus came by becoming a man. Jesus lived a sinless life. Because he lived a sinless life, He could give His own life and take the full punishment for human sin upon Himself. He did it. He gave Himself. And the pain He knew while on the cross was far beyond anything we might imagine. The physical beatings and nails and the crown were bad enough, but there was more. Much more! "God made him who had no sin to be sin for us" (2 Cor 5:21). In those moments the most incredible thing in all of history happened: Jesus literally became sin! And in His death, our sin died!

For the first time ever, the Son was separated from the Father. He cried out, "My God, my God! Why have you forsaken me?" (Matt 27:46). He had to do so, for Jesus had to die! And the Father could not watch. Jesus died, and our sin problem was solved. In His death the justice of God was satisfied, for the law was fulfilled, and in our forgiveness and His resurrection, God's mercy was also fulfilled! Praise God and the Son, who love us so much!

The Great Commission

The masses in the world know that there is a god out there somewhere; they just don't know who or where. One of the very last things that Jesus said addressed this problem. He gave the message to those first apostles and disciples—the message about a personal God who cares deeply about each individual on this little part of His creation. The message was so simple that a child could understand it: "Jesus loves me; this I know, for the Bible tells me so." Coming to Jesus was meant to be so easy that anyone could come if they just knew about Him and how to come to Him.

Note carefully that there is a great difference between being born and walking the road that He has for us. Coming to Jesus is simple; the journey requires surrender to the person and to the task.

And that is where Christians and Christianity come in! The most imposing job the world has ever seen was given to those first Christians: they were to "go into the whole world and make disciples in all the nations" (Matt 28:18-29). The world is big, and they were few! But they went, and for most of them, the price was their own lives. But they lived the promise of eternal life through Jesus, so they went.

The Bible describes this "Great Commission" several times, each time complementing the other times. In Matthew's Gospel we read, "And Jesus came and spoke to them, saying all authority has been given to me in heaven and on earth. Go therefore and disciple all the nations, baptizing them into the name of the Father and of the Son and of the Holy Spirit, teaching them to observe all that I have commanded you. And behold I am with you all the days until the consummation of the age" (Matt 28:18-20).

And then in Mark's Gospel: "And He said to them, "Go to all the world and proclaim the gospel to all creation. He who believes and is baptized shall be saved but he who does not believe shall be condemned'" (Mark 16:15-16).

Luke's Gospel also contains the words of Jesus: "And he said to them, 'Thus it is written that the Christ would suffer and would rise up from the dead on the third day, and that repentance for forgiveness of sins would be proclaimed in his name to all the nations, beginning from Jerusalem" (Luke 24:46–47).

John said it this way: "Then Jesus said to them again, 'Peace be to you; as the Father has sent me, I also send you'" (John 20:21).

And then there is one more time that we read about the Great Commission: "But you shall receive power when the Holy Spirit comes upon you, and you shall be my witnesses both in Jerusalem, and in all Judea and Samaria, and unto the uttermost part of the earth" (Acts 1:8).

The passage in Acts adds two very important things: the word for "witness" that Jesus used was the word *marturion*, which transliterates into English as "martyr." In other words, Jesus was warning that there would be a price to witness to Him in the sinful world. The second thing was that Jesus made it clear that every word spoken of Him must be in the power of the Holy Spirit (Acts 1:8).

When we put all of these passages together, we have what Christians now call "The Great Commission."

The world is in desperate need of the real Gospel of Jesus Christ. Not the Christian religion, but the real Jesus in

His people, telling the story around the world. It is being done; as Jesus said, "And this gospel of the kingdom will be preached in the whole inhabited earth for a testimony to all the nations and then the end will come" (Matt 24:14).

The Reinvention of Christianity

You may notice that I mentioned the reinvention of Christianity earlier. But I need to expand it just a bit.

In the book of Revelation, we find seven letters to seven churches. (Note that there were not seven churches in one city.) Those letters are perhaps even more important now than when they were written, for what John wrote about in the book of Revelation *we are seeing*! To the Church in Sardis, he wrote, "I know your works, that you have a name that you are alive, and yet you are dead" (Rev 3:1).

In his letter to the Thessalonians, Paul wrote, "Let no one deceive you in any way because it will not come unless the apostasy comes first" (2 Thes 2:3). The word "apostasy" comes from a compound Greek word which means "away from to stand." And it says what it means! There will come a time when many professing believers will "stand away" from things previously held tightly. There is only one standard by which Christianity can be defined accurately, and it is quite different from much of what we see of the "church" in America. Many churches in America have literally millions of dollars to spend on things such as pulpits (it is not unusual to see a pulpit that cost many thousands of dollars). I remember one time when, while attending a preacher/pastor convention, one of the host pastors stood up and bragged about his $25,000 front doors.

Churches must be judged by biblical standards and by no other way (such as outward appearances).

Doctrinally, many church groups have strayed a little from the truth. A church budget should represent two essentials: first it must represent faith, and second it must represent stewardship. Priorities must be discerned through prayer and not by the logical thinking of church members.

The virgin birth of Jesus is still an essential part of our belief system, as is His sinless life and vicarious atonement. The resurrection of Christ is critically important, for without the living Christ, we have nothing!

And then there is the return of Jesus to collect what is His! (Again, see John 14.) And there is this that Paul wrote to the Corinthians, and also to us! "For we must all appear before the judgment seat of Christ, that each one may receive the things done through the body according to what he has practiced whether good or bad" (2 Cor 5:10).

Judgment for Christians? Yes. Not for life in Heaven, but for reward or loss of reward. "If anyone's work is consumed, he will suffer loss, but he himself will be saved, yet so as through fire" (1 Cor 3:15).

I heard a churchman say, "All I want is to be saved!" That sounded OK on the surface, but it was a bit like saying to Grandma, "I really want to see you, but I don't want any of your fried chicken." It will not happen that way. If we know Him, we will want some of everything that He has prepared for us! Jesus told us that He is even now in the process of preparing a place for us! It is blatant heresy to leave this out or to change it up in any way.

So after all has been said and done, what remains? One thing above all else! We must each answer the most important question ever asked of anyone: am I ready to meet Jesus? Even the longest of life as we know it is but a blink of God's eye. Eternity is forever. God has made it possible for us to be forgiven of our sins and to have life in heaven with Him forever. The alternative is terrible beyond description, and the choice is ours! We can choose Jesus and life, or sin and death. It should be an easy choice. "Lord Jesus, I need you. I have sinned and need your forgiveness. Would you come into my life and be my own personal Lord (owner, master) and Savior (deliverer from sin and all of its consequences)?

What Is the Bible for in the Lives of Young People?

In this section we will be answering a few (out of many) questions young people ask about the Bible, prayer, the church, and many other things. The Christian life is much like natural life, in that there is birth, and then there is the living out of it. Life is difficult at best. But remember, it is more than just being born; there must be proper nourishment in order for the baby to grow. For the Christian, the Bible is the nourishment, the material needed for the life that God wants us to have.

   1. How do you study the Bible beyond just reading it? Remember, the Bible is a supernatural book written by men who were inspired by the Holy Spirit. It then must be studied under the guidance of that same Spirit. So ask Him to help you to understand. Then compare passages. The Bible is its own

interpreter. Casual reading will not do. Pray. Open the book.

2. What does it mean for the Bible to be inspired or inerrant? "Inspired" means that the Holy Spirit of God has chosen very dedicated men to write down the words that God has for us. "Inerrant" means that it is without a mistake of any kind. Note that many modern translations have taken liberties in translations and in doing so have lost some of the original meaning. The Bible is inspired the Holy Spirit. The Bible is inerrant, meaning without mistakes in its original versions. Some translations have mistakes in them.

3. What is the relationship of the Old Testament to the New Testament? The inspired book of Galatians in the New Testament has the answer. "So then the law has become our child-conductor unto faith. But since faith has come, we are no longer under a child-conductor" (Gal 3:4-5).

4. Why does the Old Testament God seem so different from the New Testament God? Of course, most of the Old Testament is the story of creation (which the New Testament verifies), the first sin (which the New Testament verifies), the law (which the

New Testament verifies), and of God's hatred of sin in any of its forms. Sin is the great destroyer of all that God loves, and that is why His attitude in the Old Testament tells us about sin and its consequences. The New Testament tells us how much the God who hates sin also loves the sinner. (Read again Galatians 3:4–5.) We must understand that the things that are sinful are also things that harm us, one way or another, and this accounts for God's attitude toward sin.

5. Why would God use Israel, the Jews, to reveal Himself? Any answer to this question would, necessarily, be speculative, so I will not speculate on it. God is God; we are not.

6. What are the theological and scientific challenges to evolution? As of this writing, the scientific challenges to evolution are becoming stronger and more numerous. Theology presents many arguments; most, if not all, are in accord with what science now knows. Evidence is everywhere for intelligent creation. The human body itself is a miracle of huge proportions. The "soup" theory is being proven impossible. If, as some evolutionists say, we were created over a period of millions of years, where are the transitional forms? An ape

did not go to sleep and wake up a man, Yet the transitional forms for evolutionary theory just are not there when there should have been thousands of them. Bible-based theology does not challenge creation, but supports it in many ways. Study the human eye. The eye is incredible in its design and in its function. Design requires a Designer! Study cell structure; study DNA. Everything that Christians believe can stand where honest evaluations are made.

7. Why doesn't God interact with us today the way He did in the periods covered in the Bible? Who says He doesn't? The difference is that we would rather say that things result from human or natural events rather than the hand of God. Humanity has moved so far away from God that people would not recognize something from Him even if He sent us special delivery mail signed "God." But He did that! The "mail" is called the Bible.

8. What does the Bible say about the exclusivity of Jesus? The Bible emphatically declares that Jesus is the *only* way to God. Jesus said it: "I am the way, the truth, and the life. No one comes to the Father but by me" (John 14:6).

9. What are some of the apparent contradictions in the Bible? As a longtime student of the Bible, I do not find contradictions; I find complementary passages. That is, sometimes it takes more than one passage to fully understand something. There are no passages that contradict the life and work of Jesus Christ. Often it takes more than one verse in order to understand what a passage is about. And if we are not careful to ask the guidance of the Holy Spirit, we may well think there is a contradiction.

10. How does a Christian approach the subject of homosexuality? Several things need to be said. First, homosexuality is not genetic, as some would have us believe. The inclination may be there to some small degree, but homosexuality is an act, not a thought. It is a choice—a bad one, but nevertheless, a choice. Is it a sin? Yes. The Bible makes it clear that God created both sexes and that the act of sex was to be consummated between a man and a woman, with no room for man to man or woman to woman. In Romans chapter one we find a very clear statement about the subject: Because of rebellion, "God gave them up to passions of dishonor, for their females exchanged the natural use for that which is contrary to nature. And likewise, also the males, leaving the natural use of the female,

burned in their craving for one another, males with males committing unseemliness, and fully receiving in themselves the retribution of their error which was due" (Rom 1:26-27).

11. But is homosexuality worse than other sins? All sin is sin; all brings judgment, and all can be fully forgiven! In that sense, all sin is involved in the judgment that Jesus suffered for us. But socially speaking, some sins are more destructive than others. Homosexuality is very, very destructive to those involved in it. As to the Christian attitude, God's love must flow through us, for "all have sinned," no exceptions.

12. What does it mean to ask God for forgiveness? We were created by God and for God. Opinions do not change that. When we rebel against the life that God has for us, we break the fellowship that we had with Him. If we know Him personally through faith in Jesus and what He did for us on the cross, we will not be happy being out of fellowship with Him. It is something we need. And when it is broken, the way back is through the prayer of confession. This means that we admit to God that we did a wrong thing, that no one else is to blame, and that we need and want to get back where we were with

Him. Honest confession is what He requires. No payment of any kind, just confession. "If we confess our sins, he is faithful to forgive us and cleanse us from all wrongdoing" (1 John 1:9). It works!

13. Why are many prayers unanswered? Most prayers are answered, but not always in the way that we wanted. God is God, and we are not. He keeps us from so many pitfalls simply because we trust Him and conclude all prayers with "not as I will, but as You will." The prayer of faith gets us through to God: "But if anyone of you lacks wisdom, let him ask of God who gives to all liberally, and does not reproach, and it will be given to him. But let him ask in faith, doubting nothing, for he who doubts is like the surge of the sea, driven by the wind and tossed about. For that man must not suppose that he will receive anything from the Lord. He is a double-minded man, unstable in all his ways" (Jas 1:5–8).

14. Why should Christians go to church? Can't you just be a Christian at home? Yes, one who knows Jesus in the pardon of sins will be a Christian at home or any place else. Church is nothing other than a group of Christians gathered together in order to 1) worship God, 2) share life with each other, and 3) be taught from the Word of God what this Christian

life is all about. And the fact is that all Christians need these three things. We don't go because of obligation; we go because we love Him and want to please Him. "Not abandoning our own assembling together as the custom of some is, but exhorting one another, and so much the more as you see the day drawing near" (Heb 10:25).

15. Why does consistency of going to church matter? It matters in the same way that consistency of eating provides nourishment for the body. If we stop eating, we die; without the spiritual food that a good church provides, we end up walking, talking dead men. We must feed both the physical and the spiritual.

16. Why does God want us to worship Him? So what is "worship?" It is the recognition that He is truly God. He wants us to know who He is. He wants us to know and experience all that He has for us. Adoration, thanksgiving, and praise are good ways to worship Him. He is our Creator, our Savior, and much more. For who He is and all that He has done and is doing, our natural response is worship. And He likes for us to respond in that way. We would too—we all like to be appreciated, especially by those whom we love.

Conclusion

So summing it all up, what is Christianity? It is nothing less and nothing more than Jesus Christ living out His life through those who have turned to Him and asked Him to forgive their sin and come into their lives as Lord and Savior. It is a very supernatural thing, and only those who have experienced it can understand it. This book has been an attempt to provide as much of an answer as this Christian writer may do. But in the last analysis, it is something that one must discover for oneself. Words, try as we may, just don't get there; personal experience is essential.

Years ago, my prayer was simple: "Lord, have mercy on me, a sinner." He heard it and answered, and to this day, seventy years later, it is still working! Try it! You will love it! God bless you!

www.ingramcontent.com/pod-product-compliance
Lightning Source LLC
LaVergne TN
LVHW052003060526
838201LV00059B/3814